TAKE GOD AT HIS WORD

EXPERIENCE THE POWER OF GIVING

Dr. Kregg Hood

SWEET
Publishing

TAKE GOD AT HIS WORD
Experience the Power of Giving

Copyright © 1996, 1998 by Sweet Publishing
3950 Fossil Creek Blvd., Suite 201
Fort Worth, TX 76137
1-800-531-5220

Scripture quotations, unless otherwise noted, are from the Holy Bible: New International Version. © 1973, 1978, 1984 by the International Bible Society. Used by permission of Zondervan Bible Publishers. Those marked KJV are from the King James Version.

ISBN: 0-8344-0271-8

Printed in the U. S. A.

98   99   00   01   02   ❖   10   9   8   7   6

CONTENTS

Giving Is a Sensitive Topic

I'll never forget the time a wealthy Christian friend told me, "Giving to the church is like pouring money down a bottomless pit; you give and give, but they're never satisfied."

Why do some Christians bristle at the mention of giving? Maybe it's because of disagreements with church leaders over how the money is spent. Maybe it's because, deep inside, we're still pretty selfish and would rather spend our money on ourselves.

But perhaps our biggest cause for concern over giving is our fear of the future. We're afraid that if we give too much away, we won't be able to make ends meet. We've all read and heard the promises in God's Word that he'll meet all of our needs. Yet we assume these passages aren't to be taken literally about physical needs. Instead, we reason that these promises must be limited to *spiritual* blessings.

The world's economy teaches us that life is uncertain and survival is difficult. But God's Word teaches us that in his economy, he always provides. The Lord owns everything, and he will generously reward his faithful, obedient children spiritually, physically, and financially, even beyond our wildest imaginations. He's just waiting for our trust.

This book invites you to take God at his word. When you do, you'll be thrilled as you discover four special words the Lord has for you. Open your heart and read on.

2 Corinthians 9:10, 11

Now he who supplies seed to the sower and bread for food will also supply and increase your store of seed and will enlarge the harvest of your righteousness. You will be made rich in every way so that you can be generous on every occasion, and through us your generosity will result in thanksgiving to God.

In the next few pages you'll discover:

- ❖ God is the source of your financial blessings.

- ❖ God gives financial rewards when you take him at his word with your giving.

- ❖ The more you give, the more you will receive.

WORD ONE:

I Will Make You Rich in Every Way

Years ago, a man was building a house in rural New England. Needing water for his new home, he commissioned an expert to dig him a well. The old well digger, seasoned in the art of his trade, scouted out the property, searching for the right spot to sink a shaft. Sure enough, he found an underground river and put in a well. Packing up his gear to leave, he left the home owner with some important advice: "Every day you must pump some water from the well. If you don't, you'll be sorry." The home owner thanked the man for the advice, and for weeks he followed the well digger's counsel and pumped water every day.

As time went on, the home owner began to take the cool, sweet water for granted. One day he left on a trip and forgot to get someone to pump water for him each day while he was away. When he returned, the water at the bottom of the well was stagnant and almost gone. He tried pumping in fresh water, but nothing came out. Later, he went to town and told the well digger his well had dried up. The old gentleman asked, "Did you remember to pump water from the well every day?" The younger man confessed his neglect and asked why this mattered. The well digger replied, "The water in the well comes from an underground river that feeds the small tributaries of water which are connected to your well. Water must continue to flow through these small tributaries so that the well can receive water. If you quit pumping the water, the ground will dry up slightly and the underground river can't find its way to your well. This cuts off the water supply." Then the old man concluded, "Remember, the source of the water is the river, not the well."[1]

If the source of your financial strength is your own personal well of resources, you risk running dry!

The Difference between Source and Means

Recognizing the difference between source and means can be tough. Our bank accounts, our abilities, and our intellects are *not* the sources of our provision and blessings. They are simply the means by which God, the Source, provides blessing. God provides for our needs according to the riches of Christ. He uses the material resources of our world as the delivery system to care for his children. To experience his abundance, we must first see him as the Source of every blessing.

Secondly, we must take him at his word because we trust that his word is true. Spiritual principles about giving relate closely to how God chooses either to bless us or to withhold his blessing. If we want our wells to contain enough resources to function effectively in our world, we must trust God and follow his teachings. The Bible teaches that giving generously out of love for God will tap you into God's unseen river of blessing.

God Will Be the Source of Your Blessing

We will improve our attitudes about giving when we recognize that God will be the source of our blessings. In Paul's thank-you note to the church at Philippi for their financial support, he says, "And my God will meet all your needs according to his glorious riches in Christ Jesus" (Philippians 4:19). Paul said God would meet every need they had. That is an awesome promise to Christians.

God's Law of the Harvest

The way we share our funds may be the most practical issue we face. Every successful farmer knows that he must sow seed if he wants to reap a crop. Scripture clearly teaches this concept. It is often referred to as the "law of the harvest." Simply stated, the more you want to reap, the more you have to sow.

This principle is first found in Genesis 8:22: "As long as the earth endures, seedtime and harvest, cold and heat, summer and winter, day and night will never cease." This passage concerns physical planting and harvest. But throughout the Bible you'll find that the law of the harvest applies to more than just the physical production of crops.

It applies to virtually every part of our lives, including man's moral behavior. "Do not be deceived: God cannot be mocked. A man reaps what he sows" (Galatians 6:7).

Another illustration of this law appears in Matthew 17. When Jesus' disciples were unable to cast out an evil spirit from a boy, he told them, "I tell you the truth, if you have faith as small as a mustard seed, you can say to this mountain, 'Move from here to there' and it will move. Nothing will be impossible for you" (vv. 20, 21). Jesus' point is clear. If you sow even a tiny amount of faith, you will reap enormous spiritual results.

The Holy Spirit guided Paul to use harvest imagery to encourage our becoming generous givers when Paul wrote, "Remember this: Whoever sows sparingly will also reap sparingly, and whoever sows generously will also reap generously" (2 Corinthians 9:6).

God Promises Rewards

Giving to the Lord is, in fact, a God-backed, guaranteed investment, not an uncertain gamble. Jesus uses the promise of reward to teach his followers. He teaches people to give without a public display because the glory should go to God, not man: "Then your Father, who sees what is done in secret, will reward you" (Matthew 6:4). God promises to reward the person who gives.

Jesus also teaches that "if anyone gives even a cup of cold water to one of these little ones because he is my disciple, . . . he will certainly not lose his reward" (Matthew 10:42). Again, the Lord reinforces a cause-and-effect relationship between giving and receiving.

The healthy desire for rewards is a legitimate motivation for Christians today. The classic text on faith, Hebrews 11:6, tells us that God "rewards those who earnestly seek him." In Matthew 6:19-34, Jesus compares giving to storing up treasures in heaven (v. 20). He tells his followers not to worry about the physical needs of life because God will take care of his children! This passage fits today, doesn't it? God longs for us to trust him enough to "seek first his kingdom and his righteousness." As we do, Jesus promises that "all these things will be given to you as well" (v. 33). "All these things" includes necessities of life such as food and clothing. Jesus gives us permission to expect God to reward his children when we trust him to provide.

God's teaching on generosity is also expressed with another principle: Trust God to reward true obedience. In general, it's easy to accept this principle in the Word of God. We see a number of examples verifying this idea throughout Scripture. We trust God to bless children who obey their parents in the Lord (Ephesians 6:1-3). We trust God to make "all things work together for good" (Romans 8:28, KJV). And we trust God to save us when we commit our lives to Jesus (Hebrews 5:9). If we didn't believe God was trustworthy in keeping his promises, there would be little point in following Jesus.

Unfortunately, many Christians act as if this principle applies in all areas of life *except* in their financial dealings. I know many Christians who are convinced that they can't afford to give to God. The reason? Fear. It's one thing to believe in God; it's another to trust God to provide the rent payment. When you're engulfed in financial hardships, it's humanly impossible to think about giving. Yet, "what is impossible with men is possible with God" (Luke 18:27). When God asks us to trust him with our finances, he also promises to reward us. He doesn't always spell out the exact ways he will repay our trust, but he does promise us a rich reward (2 Corinthians 9:11).

Also, understand that this is not what some have called the "health and wealth gospel." Any prosperity theology that attempts to turn God into some kind of genie in a bottle is merely a selfish abuse of Scripture. God has promised rewards that include financial blessings, but we must be committed to following his purpose.

Specific Rewards We're Promised

God promises his children many rewards when we give. Here are three specific rewards:

Reward 1—You will be made rich in every way.

In his letter to the Corinthian church, Paul gives an interesting definition of the word *rich:*

> Now he who supplies seed to the sower and bread for food will also supply and increase your store of seed and will enlarge the harvest of your righteousness. You will be made rich in every way so that you can be generous on every occasion, and through us your generosity will result in thanksgiving to God (2 Corinthians 9:10, 11).

God's Word defines rich as "able to be generous." God's Word also says we'll be made rich in every way. This proves we should never limit the extent of God's blessing to the spiritual or emotional arena. God promises that if we give to him, he will give us the financial capacity to be generous.

The Bible describes riches as both spiritual and material. Of all the riches we can possess, none of them is more important than spiritual riches. Scripture speaks about the riches of God's grace, God's glory, his understanding, his wisdom, and his insight. When we are generous givers, we have access to all of these riches.

Paul explains to the Corinthians that financial decisions have physical advantages as well. He isn't merely referring to the emotional or spiritual blessings we can receive from giving. He is saying that financial generosity leads to greater financial resources—even physical wealth!

This is the clear, unbiased teaching of Scripture.

However, if you have the desire to be wealthy so that you can spend these resources on yourself, don't expect to claim this reward (1 Timothy 6:9, 10). The so-called "health and wealth gospel" teaches that Christians should give to get. But God says we should give to get to give again. This, in a nutshell, is my "theology of generosity" (Titus 3:14).

I believe we have steered so far away from the ditch of the health and wealth gospel that most Christians now find themselves in the ditch on the other side of the road. We're hesitant to take God at his word and believe or teach what Scripture teaches. The text says we'll be made rich in every way, which means we'll be able to share.

I spoke with a friend who is a successful businessman and an elder in his congregation. Over the years he has counseled more than fifty couples who were in deep financial difficulty. When they came to him for advice about solving their money problems, he agreed to help if they would decide to give ten cents of every dollar they made to the Lord. My friend said every couple who followed through not only got their financial house in order, they had the opportunity to do good for God. That's a tremendous track record!

If deep in your heart you have the desire to be a good manager of God's resources and want to be generous in meeting needs so that people give thanks to God, then you *must* expect God to provide. Paul set the stage for the proper desires of our heart when he wrote, "For you know the grace of our Lord Jesus Christ, that though he was rich, yet for your sakes he became poor, so that you through his poverty might become rich" (2 Corinthians 8:9). It's difficult to twist the Scriptures into a selfish interpretation when you keep the focus on Jesus!

God doesn't oppose blessing his servants with material

well-being, as long as they keep their desires and fortunes devoted to him. First Chronicles 29:12 tells us that wealth comes from God. Passages like Joshua 1:8; Proverbs 3:9, 10; and Malachi 3:10 will help us overcome our fears about God's provision.

The Old Testament clearly tells us that God made people like Abraham, Jacob, David, Solomon, Jehoshaphat, and Job wealthy. In the New Testament we read of wealthy followers of God, like Joseph of Arimathea, Lydia, and others. If there were no wealthy Christians, there would be no need for this kind of teaching. If God hated material wealth, why would he grant physical riches as a reward to many of his people? God wants to reward his faithful, generous followers with both spiritual and material riches. I believe this is true because it is taught in God's Word.

Reward 2—You will receive more than you give.

When was the last time you read Luke 6:38? "Give, and it will be given to you. A good measure, pressed down, shaken together and running over, will be poured into your lap. For with the measure you use, it will be measured to you." I have a confession to make. For far too long I have simply not believed this passage. I have tried hard to find some way to get around the truth that is taught so clearly. I think my motivation was based partially on my opposition to what some call "prosperity teaching." But, deep inside, I think my struggles with this passage really signaled my lack of faith in God to reward my obedient giving.

Jesus says to tap into God's economy. The Lord is a generous provider. You won't run out of money! Don't be afraid to give. When you give, you also receive—"a good measure, pressed down, shaken together and running over, will be poured into your lap." I've never seen an exception to this rule. You always receive more than you give. If you give love, you receive more love. If you give friendship, you receive more friends in return. I've even noticed if you give a smile to someone, you will receive more smiles. So it follows from Scripture and practical experience that if you give money, you receive more money.

For years I struggled with this text. I thought it was materialistic to think God would bless me financially when I gave money to do his work. But, in reality, the materialistic view is thinking that my own ingenuity is the only source of my ability to make money. A spiritual person obeys and trusts God to release his blessings and provide all the resources of life. The unspiritual person believes human effort is the source of material wealth.

Reward 3—You will receive a greater blessing.

Acts 20:35 shares a familiar quotation of our Lord: "It is more blessed to give than to receive." We all agree that it's a blessing to receive, but Jesus says it's an even greater blessing to *give*! However enjoyable you think receiving is, Jesus says giving is better—it is more blessed.

I've pondered Jesus' statement for years. How could giving bring a greater blessing? This made no sense to me, especially as a young child. Like most kids, I always hoped for a big haul under the tree on Christmas morning. I had my wish list and was never bashful about sharing it with my parents. My mother's standard reply to my childish, greedy nature was to quote Acts 20:35. It's no wonder I never cared much for that verse when I was a kid!

Now that I'm a parent, I've gained a fuller understanding about Jesus' teaching. First, I receive a greater blessing by helping someone and seeing their excitement or appreciation. Second, I receive a greater blessing by realizing God has given me something to share. What if I were the one in need? Having something to share creates feelings of gratitude for God's provision. Third, I receive a greater blessing because I have something else to look forward to. Giving allows me to participate in God's economy, where my financial investments in his kingdom generate remarkable returns.

A preacher friend of mine has a quick, three-point outline on giving that he drew from Galatians 6:7. He says: (1) You reap what you sow; (2) you reap more than you sow; and (3) you reap after you sow. When I use this scripture to see the way God works, I see giving in a different light. Giving is not an expense, it's an opportunity!

Receive Blessings "In Kind"

Both common sense and these passages imply that the type of seed you sow determines the kind of crop you will receive. If you sow corn, you will reap corn (Genesis 8:22). If you sow moral actions in your daily behavior, you will reap a moral life (Galatians 6:7). If you sow faith, you will reap faith (Matthew 17:20). If you sow financially, you will reap financially (2 Corinthians 9:6).

This teaching is well represented throughout the Bible. If you sow obedience to the gospel, you reap eternal life. If you sow Bible study, you reap spiritual insight. In Scripture, there is an exact match between the kind of thing you sow and the kind of thing you reap. This same cause-and-effect principle applies to judging, condemning, and forgiving (Luke 6:37). Jesus promises "a good measure, pressed down, shaken together and running over" (v. 38). Jesus wants us to know not only that we receive more than we give, but that we receive the same kind of thing that we give. So Jesus tells us that the amount and kind of gift we *give* determines the amount and kind of gift we *receive*. I have found *no exception* in Scripture to this insight.

Trust God to Provide

God's Word calls us to have faith in his promises. If we see him as the source of our blessings, we won't be afraid of running out of the physical resources we need. When you are facing too much month at the end of your money, remember God's promise to provide for your needs—and more.

One of the most fantastic accounts of God's provision comes from 2 Kings 4:1-7. A poor widow came to Elisha the prophet and cried out to him in despair. Creditors were threatening to take away her two sons as slaves to pay her debts. When Elisha asked what resources she possessed, the woman replied that all she had was a small amount of oil. Elisha told her to go to all her neighbors and borrow as many of their empty jars as she could get. Then she was to go inside and start pouring oil from her jar into the empty jars. Her sons brought jars to her, and she kept pouring until all the jars were full. When she poured her oil into the last jar, the oil stopped flowing. Elisha then told her to sell the oil to pay her debts and live on what was left.

Not only did God provide for her, but the amount of God's provision was in direct proportion to her trust. He gave her as much oil as she was prepared to receive. And God will provide material blessings to meet our physical needs and gain our spiritual attention as well.

God's response to money problems is the same as his answer to health concerns, family problems, or any other difficult circumstances. God wants us to trust *him*, not our job or our bank balance. Jesus said, "For where your treasure is, there your heart will be also" (Matthew 6:21). Since God wants our hearts, he works through our finances. When we learn to trust him with our money, we will learn to trust him with anything—even our very lives!

Notes:

1Adapted from *God Is Able* by Elmer Towns and John Maxwell (Lynchburg, VA: Church Growth Institute, 1986). Used by permission.

Think It Through
Word One: I Will Make You Rich in Every Way

1. Listed below are several of the resources commonly used to provide for the daily necessities of life. Which one do you depend on the most? Why?

Job	Savings	Education
Who you know	Intellect	Good luck
Investments	Parents	Land
Appearance	Personality	Other:

2. What would you do if your primary resource was suddenly taken away?

3. Read the following passages and identify the general theme of each one.

Passage	Theme
Joshua 1:8	
Malachi 3:9-11	
Proverbs 3:9, 10	
Luke 6:38	

Compare your answer for question 1 to these themes. Do your responses match?

4. If you were to see God as the true source of your blessings, what would be the first financial decision you would make?

Meditate on God's Word

Take God at his word, and let the truths of these texts convince you that he will provide for you materially.

Joshua 1:8

Do not let this Book of the Law depart from your mouth; meditate on it day and night, so that you may be careful to do everything written in it. Then you will be prosperous and successful.

Luke 12:29

And do not set your heart on what you will eat or drink; do not worry about it.

Luke 12:31

But seek his kingdom, and these things will be given to you as well.

Philippians 4:6

Do not be anxious about anything, but in everything, by prayer and petition, with thanksgiving, present your requests to God.

Philippians 4:17-19

Not that I am looking for a gift, but I am looking for what may be credited to your account. I have received full payment and even more; I am amply supplied, now that I have received from Epaphroditus the gifts you sent. They are a fragrant offering, an acceptable sacrifice, pleasing to God. And my God will meet all your needs according to his glorious riches in Christ Jesus.

1 Timothy 6:17, 18

Command those who are rich in this present world not be be arrogant nor to put their hope in wealth, which is so uncertain, but to put their hope in God, who richly provides us with everything for our enjoyment. Command them to do good, to be rich in good deeds, and to be generous and willing to share.

Are you excited about this journey of faith you've read about? Ponder the possibilities and confirm your decision to trust God's word as you pray.

Let's Pray ...

Lord, I pause to proclaim to you that I know you are the Sovereign Ruler of this universe. I also know you are aware of all my needs. You are the source of all my blessings, too. But I need your help so that I can trust you and tap in to the rewards you promise through your law of the harvest. I want to be blessed so I can bless others in your name. I will take you at your word and make a commitment to obey the Scriptures. I will also wait with anticipation to see what you will do next because of Jesus. In his name. Amen.

Malachi 3:10

"Bring the whole tithe into the storehouse, that there may be food in my house. Test me in this," says the LORD *Almighty, "and see if I will not throw open the floodgates of heaven and pour out so much blessing that you will not have room enough for it."*

In the next few pages you'll discover:

❖ God invites us to take him at his word and test him by tithing.

❖ Tithing is a doorway to God's blessings today.

❖ If you don't tithe, you may fall "under a curse"!

WORD TWO:

I Want You to Tithe So I Can Reward You

Throughout the years, God has released great blessings when his children wholeheartedly followed him. If you "honor the LORD with your wealth, with the firstfruits of all your crops; then your barns will be filled to overflowing, and your vats will brim over with new wine" (Proverbs 3:9, 10). What a great promise from Scripture! Do you realize that this inspired promise still applies to us today? Deciding to make your tithe a *starting point* in your giving allows God the opportunity he's looking for to bless you in ways he would not otherwise.

The Book of Malachi reveals how important the tithe is to God. When his people refused to honor him with their wealth, God actually accused them of stealing from him:

"Will a man rob God? Yet you rob me.

"But you ask, 'How do we rob you?'

"In tithes and offerings. You are under a curse—the whole nation of you—because you are robbing me. Bring the whole tithe into the storehouse, that there may be food in my house. Test me in this," says the LORD Almighty, "and see if I will not throw open the floodgates of heaven and pour out so much blessing that you will not have room enough for it" (3:8-10).

God's Word says that when his people obeyed him by tithing, he would shower them with material blessing. But when they refused to follow his wishes regarding their giving, the Bible says they fell "under a curse"!

Sometimes, Christians get swept up in a debate over whether or not we're *required* to tithe, when that's not the real question. The real question is, does the *promise* of Malachi 3:9, 10 still apply today? I believe it does.

I have yet to find any passage in the New Testament that rescinded this promise, just as I have found no New Testament passage that ever rescinded God's rainbow promise about a flood.

Do you believe God will never destroy the earth by water again? How do you know? Your confidence is certainly based on the promise found in Genesis 9:12-16. In that passage God said,

This is the sign of the covenant I am making between me and you and every living creature with you, a covenant for all generations to come: I have set my rainbow in the clouds, and it will be the sign of the covenant between me and the earth. When-ever I bring clouds over the earth and the rainbow appears in the clouds, I will remember my covenant between me and you and all living creatures of every kind. Never again will the waters become a flood to destroy all life. Whenever the rainbow appears in the clouds, I will see it and remember the everlasting covenant between God and all living creatures of every kind on the earth.

This promise did not have to be restated in the New Testament in order to be valid today, just as the promise of Proverbs 3:5, 6 about guidance did not have to be restated. God's promise in regard to tithing is no different. Our decision to give 10 percent of our income back to God reflects our reliance on him as the source of all our blessings. This kind of faith pleases the Lord and brings abundant blessing.

Let's not fall prey to "legalistic righteousness" and require the New Testament to command us to tithe before we use this simple measure as a generosity standard. We could miss many of God's richest blessings if we refuse to take him at his word.

Power Principles of Tithing

Both biblical principles and practical experiences demonstrate the power of tithing in a Christian's life. Since God's Word repeatedly uses the sowing and reaping illustration to encourage giving back to him, it's a powerful exercise to see what will happen when we take him at his word and tithe as a starting point for giving. What will we reap?

I've discovered four awesome, biblical principles of tithing.

Power Principle 1— Tithing motivates greater faithfulness.

Did you know that Jesus actually taught his followers to live by a higher standard than the one given in the Old

Testament? Obviously, we, too, want to please him and be faithful to his call. Jesus contrasted the requirements of the Law with the plan for his followers.

The following chart cites several examples and raises the question, Which is the higher standard, the Law of Moses or the Way of Christ?

Old Testament	New Testament
Do not murder. (Exodus 20:13)	Anyone who hates his brother is a murderer. (1 John 3:15)
Do not commit adultery. (Exodus 20:14)	Anyone who lusts commits adultery in his heart. (Matthew 5:28)
Do not swear falsely by God's name. (Leviticus 19:12)	Do not swear at all. (Matthew 5:34)
The entire tithe will be holy to the LORD. (Leviticus 27:32)	Give as you are prospered. (1 Corinthians 16:2)

An exhaustive study of the Scriptures reveals this often overlooked truth: Jesus' way *always* calls for greater faithfulness and commitment than was required in the Old Testament. Can giving *possibly* be an exception? It follows clearly that no one who wants to be faithful to God would ever think of doing less than the Old Testament believers. Remember, Christ came to fulfill the Law, not to destroy it (Matthew 5:17). And Hebrews 10:1 says, "The law is only a shadow of the good things that are coming—not the realities themselves."

Jesus came to bring us "the good things." If we want these things in our life, then we must sow the seed necessary to reap them. His Word teaches that faithfulness in tithing is one of the pathways to receiving the spiritual and physical blessings he desires for us.

It amazed me when I learned that tithing was not unique to God's chosen people! Other ancient civilizations also practiced giving a tenth of their income to various pagan deities. Archaeological research indicates that the people of Egypt, Babylon, and Assyria also tithed. Imagine that! Both Jewish followers of God and pagans devoted to false deities saw that spiritual faithfulness included tithing.

Dr. John Willis, a distinguished professor of Old Testament studies, has written a profound paper on tithing. In it he says:

> By giving their tithes, the Israelites were proclaiming that they were giving back to the Lord a portion of that which he had prospered them (Deuteronomy 26:10-15). Just as God had given his people the food and resources they needed for their existence, by tithing the people were imitating him by giving their God-given food and resources to the slaves, the poor, the sojourners, the orphans, and the widows. Thus, tithing was the means God gave the Israelites to express their love to God for all he had given them (Deuteronomy 6:4-9) and to express their love to their neighbor as God had expressed his love to them (Leviticus 19:18).[1]

Surely, as recipients of "the good things," it's also clear that the Lord has commissioned us to do the same today!

Power Principle 2—Tithing releases God's financial blessings!

Malachi 3:10 says, " 'Bring the whole tithe into the

storehouse, that there may be food in my house. Test me in this,' says the LORD Almighty, 'and see if I will not throw open the floodgates of heaven and pour out so much blessing that you will not have room enough for it.' " This is one of the most remarkable passages in the whole Bible. The God of the universe actually told his people to test him. The Hebrew word for *test* means "to examine." God said they could check him out and see if he was telling the truth. This is the only time in Scripture when God allowed his creation to see if he really would keep his word. The Lord told them that if they would once again put him first and prove their loyal devotion to him by bringing in their whole tithe, he would drench them with material blessings. They could go to the bank on this promise!

I am convinced God will do the same today. I know many people who have taken God at his word and tithed when they didn't know how they possibly could. One Christian I know of who had never tithed before started tithing, and, for no apparent reason, his business quadrupled. He said he believed God was the source of his blessing because he hadn't changed any of his business practices. In fact, this man was even working fewer hours.

What if you are financially strapped? One of the young, single-parent moms in a church I preached for determined to tithe, even though she couldn't cover her current monthly expenses. She signed a pledge card, not knowing where the money would come from. Two days later her boss called her into his office unexpectedly. He praised her work and gave her a 13 percent raise on the spot! While excited about the raise, she was overjoyed at the realization that God had come through!

Now, after years of listening to the faith stories of others, I have yet to hear of a single story where God did not abundantly bless obedient, grateful love like this. Just remember, we don't give to *be* blessed, we give because we *are* blessed. Tithing declares our realization that God has already blessed us, as well as our conviction that he will continue to take care of us.

Power Principle 3—Tithing expands Kingdom work.

The average percentage of Christian giving is only 2.5 percent. It doesn't take a mathematical genius to see that churchwide tithing would allow ministry efforts to virtually explode. Imagine how much greater God would be glorified if the kingdom of Christ quadrupled its resources! You allow God to have a greater influence in the world around you when you honor him with your financial tithe.

I've preached as a guest speaker in a congregation that only two years ago was struggling to pay the bills. They began to emphasize taking God at his word and strongly encouraged the members to begin tithing. In a matter of weeks, their giving boomed and the morale in the church skyrocketed. New plans and ministries began to sprout, involvement increased dramatically, and the ministry impact on the community expanded with a fresh vision. They continued to stretch, and now their weekly budget is almost twice what it was before they realized the link between trusting God and giving. This is now an excited church! Tithing provides abundant resources to do ministry.

Power Principle 4—Tithing changes spending habits.

If your giving standard has been low, starting to tithe may seem to stretch you financially at first. But in the process of tithing, you learn to prioritize your spending patterns and develop a sound financial budget. This will allow you more money to give. You'll also find that the discipline brought on by tithing will help you fight the materialistic urges prompted by the marketing gurus of our consumer-driven society.

People who are committed to tithing evaluate their spending habits more closely. They follow spiritually and financially healthy practices which protect their ability to trust God to provide for them. These practices include setting aside their weekly offering first, making purchasing decisions in light of how those decisions will impact their offering to the Lord, and thinking about what they really need versus what they think they need. It's a lot like establishing a good nutrition plan. When you eat right, you stay healthier and happier. In the same way, when you establish a solid commitment to tithe you will trim the fat out of your spending, leaving more for the Kingdom and more for you to spend wisely.

Living under a Curse

The other side of this opportunity is a question: What happens if you don't take God at his word in tithing? To see what can happen, look at the Book of Malachi. Chapters one through three of Malachi showed the wicked state of affairs in Israel. The hearts of the people and their priests were corrupt. They were plagued with sin, divorce, and social injustice. Malachi 3:9 reveals that they were under a curse simply because they failed to honor God with their tithe.

These are chilling words. The Bible uses the word *curse* to describe the fruit of their unfaithfulness toward God and his purposes for them. The grammatical structure of this phrase in Hebrew is even more shocking. This passage says literally that God's people were "cursed with a curse." When you look at the definition of *curse* and see how it's used in other passages in the Scripture, it's clear that it refers to the experience of God either bringing punishment or withholding blessing. For example, Malachi 2:2 says, "'If you do not listen, and if you do not set your heart to honor my name,' says the LORD Almighty, 'I will send a curse upon you, and I will curse your blessings. Yes, I have already cursed them, because you have not set your heart to honor me.'"

Think of the many ways that you could be "under a curse" and having to endure a situation that you know is not God's best. Perhaps your relationship with a loved one is in shambles, or your business opportunities seem extremely limited. Or it could be that Jesus doesn't seem real to you. On the other hand, wouldn't you like to experience the favor of God in your life? God clearly pronounces both spiritual and physical blessings on those who follow his will. God's blessings affect life's happiness, finances, government, longevity of life, and our eternal destination.

The following passages give you a brief sample of how God withholds curses and releases blessings.

Psalm 128:1-4

Blessed are all who fear the LORD, who walk in his ways. You will eat the fruit of your labor; blessings and prosperity will be yours. Your wife will be like a fruitful vine within your house; your sons will be like olive shoots around your table. Thus is the man blessed who fears the LORD.

Proverbs 10:22

The blessing of the LORD brings wealth, and he adds no trouble to it.

Proverbs 11:11

Through the blessing of the upright a city is exalted, but by the mouth of the wicked it is destroyed.

Ephesians 6:1-3

> Children, obey your parents in the Lord, for this is right. "Honor your father and mother"—which is the first commandment with a promise—"that it may go well with you and that you may enjoy long life on the earth."

James 1:12

> Blessed is the man who perseveres under trial, because when he has stood the test, he will receive the crown of life that God has promised to those who love him.

If there is an area in your life where you continually feel defeated, maybe it's time to see if that problem is caused by your inattention to the promises of God which are linked to your being able to receive a blessing. That is exactly what Malachi was trying to communicate.

It's also why I believe curses still occur today. A brilliant, young electrical engineer, whose life was in trouble, wrote a letter telling about his experience. Here's an excerpt that I have received permission to share:

> As you know, I came to this church a very hurting person. I carried burdens that left me completely helpless. I was existing, but not really living. Three years ago I grew gravely ill and lost most of my physical strength and much of my immune system. At my lowest point, I literally crawled across my front lawn to get to my car because I was too weak to walk. I felt that I was dying, and I was morbidly afraid of death and literally terrified of going to hell. I was out of touch with God. I felt if I could just find another doctor surely everything would get better.
>
> Then, in desperation, without asking for anything

specific, I cried out to God to help me. "Please God," I prayed, "Do something to let me know you're here." I was ready to do anything. Now I know that God was humbling me so that I would come to trust him more completely.

On my first visit to [church], I was astonished! Even though this congregation is very large, I felt comfortable here immediately. I felt a keen sense of the presence of God which I had never felt anywhere else. [The minister] is an inspired preacher. His sermons are always helpful, but the moment of truth came when he preached a sermon on stewardship and said, "Anyone who does not give back to God 10 percent of his income is a thief." I had never even seriously thought of giving 10 percent and couldn't imagine how in the world that could possibly fit into my tight budget.

But the word "thief" hit me hard as the truth always does. I now realize that I was so miserable precisely because *God was last on my list of priorities rather than first.* So I asked God's forgiveness, and I pledged to give back 10 percent of my income for the rest of my life. This is the most important decision I have ever made.

From that moment, things began to change dramatically for the better. The people who are closest to me have marveled at the changes in my life. Too many positive things have happened to be coincidence. Most obvious is my greatly improved health, which has been immediate. Most practical is that, after looking for a job for three years, I found one—the best job I've ever had in my life! Most gratifying is the deep feeling of inner peace, which, for the first time in my life, I feel. I feel different on the inside than when I first came to see you, and everybody who knows me says I'm different on the outside, too.

What a story! If you're experiencing great financial difficulty, have you considered the possibility that you might be living under a curse? The Word of God is full of texts that show how disobeying God leads to a number of curses. Failing to tithe places you in just as much risk of a curse as committing more familiar and obvious sins, such as refusing to repent, disrespecting parents, stealing, or lying.

The principle of tithing is simple. If you tithe you will receive God's blessings. If you don't tithe you *rob God*, and you *cheat yourself.*

God releases his power when we put our faith in him. Take him at his word, and he will respond with blessing. The Word says:

> If any of you lacks wisdom, he should ask God, who gives generously to all without finding fault, and it will be given to him. But when he asks, he must believe and not doubt, because he who doubts is like a wave of the sea, blown and tossed by the wind. That man should not think he will receive anything from the Lord; he is a double-minded man, unstable in all he does (James 1:5-8).

Avoid double-minded thinking. Let faith take charge of your heart as you take hold of God's promises. It's not a matter of whether or not you can afford to tithe, it's whether or not you can afford not to. When you put the Lord first, he promises to open up heaven and pour out his blessings.

Notes:

[1]John T. Willis, Ph.D., "Tithing and Other Kinds of Giving in the Old Testament." Used by permission.

Think It Through
Word Two: I Want You to Tithe So I May Reward You

1. Read each passage about God's kingdom and contrast it with the world's mind-set:

    1 Chronicles 29:12

    Psalm 50:9, 10

    Proverbs 3:9, 10

    Proverbs 10:22

    1 Timothy 6:6-10

2. If someone were to ask you for advice about tithing, what would you tell them?

3. How did the story about the young engineer (pages 26 and 27) make you feel? Why?

4. Why don't you "put God to the test" (Malachi 3:10)?

Meditate on God's Word

God already owns everything, so why does he want us to give? These passages reveal his desire for us to trust him for all our needs and to desire to be generous like him. As you read these texts, ask yourself if your thinking reflects the mind-set of this world or of God's kingdom.

Deuteronomy 8:17, 18

You may say to yourself, "My power and the strength of my hands have produced this wealth for me." But remember the LORD your God, for it is he who gives you the ability to produce wealth, and so confirms his covenant, which he swore to your forefathers, as it is today.

Proverbs 3:9, 10

Honor the LORD with your wealth,
　　with the firstfruits of all your crops;
then your barns will be filled to overflowing,
　　and your vats will brim over with new wine.

2 Chronicles 31:5

As soon as the order went out, the Israelites generously gave the firstfruits of their grain, new wine, oil and honey and all that the fields produced. They brought a great amount, a tithe of everything.

Malachi 3:6-12

"I the LORD do not change. So you, O descendants of Jacob, are not destroyed. Ever since the time of your forefathers you have turned away from my decrees and have not kept them. Return to me, and I will return to you," says the LORD Almighty.

"But you ask, 'How are we to return?'

"Will a man rob God? Yet you rob me.

"But you ask, 'How do we rob you?'

"In tithes and offerings. You are under a curse—the whole nation of you—because you are robbing me. Bring the whole tithe into the storehouse, that there may be food in my house. Test me in this," says the LORD Almighty, "and see if I will not throw open the floodgates of heaven and pour out so much blessing that you will not have room enough for it. I will prevent pests from devouring your crops, and the vines in your fields will not cast their fruit," says the LORD Almighty. "Then all the nations will call you blessed, for yours will be a delightful land," says the LORD Almighty.

Matthew 5:20

For I tell you that unless your righteousness surpasses that of the Pharisees and the teachers of the law, you will certainly not enter the kingdom of heaven.

Luke 6:38

Give, and it will be given to you. A good measure, pressed down, shaken together and running over, will be poured into your lap. For with the measure you use, it will be measured to you.

Galatians 6:9

Let us not become weary in doing good, for at the proper time we will reap a harvest if we do not give up.

Philippians 4:12-19

I know what it is to be in need, and I know what it is to have plenty. I have learned the secret of being content in any and every situation, whether well fed or hungry, whether living in plenty or in want. I can do everything through him who gives me strength.

Yet it was good of you to share in my troubles. Moreover, as you Philippians know, in the early days of your acquaintance with the gospel, when I set out from Macedonia, not one church shared with me in the matter of giving and receiving, except you only; for even when I was in Thessalonica, you sent me aid again and again when I was in need. Not that I am looking for a gift, but I am looking for what may be credited to your account. I have received full payment and even more; I am amply supplied, now that I have received from Epaphroditus the gifts you sent. They are a fragrant offering, an acceptable sacrifice, pleasing to God. And my God will meet all your needs according to his glorious riches in Christ Jesus.

Hebrews 13:5, 16

Keep your lives free from the love of money and be content with what you have, because God has said,

> "Never will I leave you;
> never will I forsake you."

And do not forget to do good and to share with others, for with such sacrifices God is pleased.

God's promises are exciting and amazing. Are you ready to "test him" by tithing? Decide now to stand on his revealed promises and pray with assurance that he is listening closely to your words...and your heart.

Let's Pray ...

Holy Father, you have humbled me today. I honor you with my words of devotion and trust, but I must confess that the pull of the world's economic system is strong. Help me put my full weight down on your promises to "throw open the floodgates of heaven and pour out so much blessing" that I truly do not have room for it. That is hard for me to believe, but with the power of your risen Son working in my heart, I will trust and obey! Thank you in advance for what you will do because you love me. In Jesus' name. Amen.

1 Timothy 6:17-19

Command those who are rich in this present world not to be arrogant nor to put their hope in wealth, which is so uncertain, but to put their hope in God, who richly provides us with everything for our enjoyment. Command them to do good, to be rich in good deeds, and to be generous and willing to share. In this way they will lay up treasure for themselves as a firm foundation for the coming age, so that they may take hold of life that is truly life.

In the next few pages you'll discover:

❖ God owns everything; you are one of his managers.

❖ Giving "tithes and offerings" ensures your continued reception of God's blessings.

❖ Being a generous manager of God's resources shows your quality of love for him.

WORD THREE:

I Trust You to Manage Material Resources

There are three types of givers. The first is like flint. You have to strike it to get it to produce a spark. The second is like a sponge because you have to squeeze it to get it to turn loose of what's inside. The third is like a honeycomb. Its contents just ooze out all over!

Which one best describes you? If you want to experience God's blessing, you'll be like the honeycomb and let your resources flow out as a part of your nature. And you'll put God in control of your finances.

First, it is vital to understand a key money management principle: God owns everything (Psalm 50:10). Everything we possess is merely on loan from him so that we can use his resources to bring him glory and expand his kingdom. He has given us the abilities we have to make a living

(Deuteronomy 8:17, 18). Understanding that I have the honor of managing some of his material resources has also helped me see that I can take God at his word.

Since we are managers, it follows that we should follow the instructions of our Owner. One of God's important principles is, "Whoever can be trusted with very little can also be trusted with much." This passage in Luke 16:10 shows us that the Lord entrusts more and more of his material resources to us as we prove we can be trusted to manage them effectively. This is one of the reasons why God has always wanted his people to be generous in giving money to do work that pleases him. It's a form of spiritual resource management.

Throughout the Bible, God's people made offerings in order to support ministry projects and programs, like the famine relief to Jerusalem (Romans 15:25, 26) and the care of widows (1 Timothy 5:16). God's people also gave to construct and maintain facilities for worship (Exodus 25:1-8; 2 Kings 12:5). Throughout both Testaments, the Lord's faithful contributed money to support the physical needs of leaders, teachers, and workers in God's service (Deuteronomy 18:1; Philippians 4:15; 1 Timothy 5:17, 18).

The spirit of boundless generosity flows throughout the Old and New Testament scriptures. Two passages illustrate this well—Exodus 36:4-7 and 2 Corinthians 8:3-5. They both reveal the giving heart God seeks.

> So all the skilled craftsmen who were doing all the work on the sanctuary left their work and said to Moses, "The people are bringing more than enough for doing the work the LORD commanded to be done."
>
> Then Moses gave an order and they sent this word throughout the camp: "No man or woman is to make anything else as an offering for the sanctuary." And so

the people were restrained from bringing more, because what they already had was more than enough to do all the work (Exodus 36:4-7).

For I testify that they gave as much as they were able, and even beyond their ability. Entirely on their own, they urgently pleaded with us for the privilege of sharing in this service to the saints.

And they did not do as we expected, but they gave themselves first to the Lord and then to us in keeping with God's will (2 Corinthians 8:3-5).

God wants his people to experience the privilege of giving—even those in poverty. All financial decisions are actually spiritual decisions. And when we put God first in our giving, we are involved in an act of worship to the Almighty.

It's Time to Decide

Do you long for the opportunity to worship God with wholehearted devotion? Do you give generously for a couple of weeks, then start slacking off gradually? Remember, Satan is very clever. He stops at nothing to keep you from taking God at his word, from trusting him to reward your faithfulness. Make the following *three specific decisions*, no matter what your financial situation might be, and Satan will fail! God will ensure your success because he is the source of your blessing!

Decision 1—Give to the Lord this Sunday.

Make this Sunday the day you take a bold step of faith, and follow God with your finances. First Corinthians provides specific, helpful insight. "Now about the collection for God's people: Do what I told the Galatian churches to do. On the first day of every week, each one of you should set aside a sum of money in keeping with his income, saving it up, so that when I come no collections will have to be made" (16:1, 2).

Paul leaves no room for doubt. Everyone is to be involved because everyone has some kind of income. Even children can give a portion of their allowances to do God's work. Children who learn to give when they're young will grow up trusting the Lord with their finances. Just think of how many debt and spending traps they will avoid!

Decision 2–Give to the Lord every Sunday.

Since Paul is responding to their questions about when and how to give, these instructions also give wise counsel about the frequency of giving. Paul's inspired wisdom also tells us to give "on the first day of every week" (v. 2). Paul wanted their offerings "stored up" so no special collections would be necessary after he arrived. He knew the power of saving. A larger gift would be possible if the people set aside money regularly. Plus, the people were building a healthy, spiritual habit.

Decision 3–Plan to give "tithes and offerings."

When Paul tells the church at Corinth to "set aside a sum of money in keeping with his income," he gives no legislated amount for the Christian to give. There's no statement about percentages or specific monetary figures in any of the New Testament passages. But remember, the Old Testament was written "to teach us" (Romans 15:4) and thoroughly equip us for every good work (2 Timothy 3:17). In the Old Testament the primary use of the tithe was to support the priests and on-going worship activities of the people of God. Their offerings were given in addition to their tithes and were used for special purposes.

This Old Testament principle of "tithes and offerings" is

an effective biblical way to develop your own giving plan today. Some priorities should receive attention in your plan:

Give to the Lord first. This idea of firstfruits is found in Proverbs 3:9, 10. It teaches that giving the first part of the crop as it came in was a sign of trust in the Lord's provision. The Israelites had no way of knowing on their own if the rest of the crop would come in. They had to trust God. This text says they would receive a great harvest if they honored God with their wealth.

Several years ago I was talking with a young man about giving. He shared the struggles he and his wife had about giving, despite his good job. Typically, they waited until late in the month to write their offering check. Like most young couples, they were usually strapped for funds by the end of the month, having little left for the Lord's work.

I know how easily couples can fall into this situation, so I casually mentioned how my wife and I give 10 percent. We literally write our checks to the church first, even before our house payment. Even though I am paid twice a month, we write four checks because we want to stay in the habit of making weekly offerings. I told him that this figure is built into our budget. I found out later that this young man went home that night and told his wife about our discussion. They decided to start writing out their offerings before they wrote any other checks. Giving the "firstfruits" of their income allowed both their offering and their faith to grow dramatically.

Tithe to your home congregation. In the Old Testament, God wanted the center of Jewish worship and spiritual leadership strong. God's people brought their tithes and offerings to the priests (Deuteronomy 12:5, 6). This practice parallels the teaching of 1 Corinthians 16:2, where the church contributions were "set aside" and used for ministry. Today, as well, your home congregation needs to be strong. It's where you receive the greatest blessing. It's where your kids go to Sunday school, where your ministry has its greatest focus, and where you share in your closest friendships. It's where you're most involved and receive the greatest spiritual nurturing. When you give to bless your home congregation, you, in turn, are blessed in many ways.

Give extra offerings as the Lord prompts your heart. Don't ever feel bound to stop at giving 10 percent. Our goal should be to "excel in this grace of giving" (2 Corinthians 8:7). Sometimes you have more to give and sometimes you have less. What should you do? Another Old Testament example says, "Tell the Israelites to bring me an offering. You are to receive the offering for me from each man whose heart prompts him to give" (Exodus 25:2). This passage, from God's instructions on the building of the tabernacle, illustrates the Lord's desire to see us choose to give more when there's a special reason. In the Exodus story the people gave so much that Moses had to tell them to stop. This extravagant response to God's work is important today, too.

I have another good friend who has tithed for a number of years. About a year and a half ago, he and his wife felt convicted to go beyond tithing and give additional offerings. The Lord honored their faith in a marvelous way. First, God helped them to change their attitudes toward money and spending. They stopped focusing on their own pleasures and started looking for ways to serve God with the resources he entrusted to them.

Secondly, my friend saw a remarkable thing happen that year. Even though he was less busy, his income literally tripled! He is now convinced that God tries to find good people he can use by giving them money. This couple has learned that many Christians don't have enough simply because they don't give enough. Giving offerings above the tithe is a specific way to take Jesus at his word. They are receiving a blessing that is "pressed down, shaken together and running over."

One of the most frequent times when offerings are important occurs during a church building project. Effective, spiritually motivated churches shy away from making this time a mere fund raising experience. Instead, they ask their members to pray about "what God wants to give through them." Since God already owns everything, what could be a more accurate way of looking at giving?

Del Rogers, one of my friends who has helped thousands of churches with capital stewardship campaigns, encourages people to pray and seek God's will before making a decision during a capital stewardship campaign. Over the years he has heard many wonderful stories of personal financial commitment. You might find one of these ideas lights a spark in your heart, too:

> "We purchased a piece of land years ago and are going to give that piece of land to the church to be sold for our new building, as a gift up front, then we will give sacrificially and regularly over the next 156 weeks."

> "We have been saving for a new home. We have decided to put that off for the next three years and give what we would have paid as a down payment and the extra monthly payments to our church for God's house, rather than our own."

> "We are going to put off buying a new car in order that we might increase our commitment. We will give what the new car payments plus interest would have been to the Lord's house."

"We have decided to sacrifice some social activities in order to increase our weekly commitment."

"We usually go out as a family twice a week to eat at nice restaurants and spend $50-$60 a meal. We are going to give up one of those meals and give that money, above what our commitment was going to be, as our sacrifice for our new building."

"We are not going on vacation this year in order to increase our commitment."

"We are going to double our tithing and give the second tithe to the building so that we can share the vision."[1]

It's truly amazing what people have the courage to do after they pray!

For me it's actually fun to give extra offerings. Karen and I pray for wisdom and the resources to share in what God is doing through us. Then we choose special benevolence needs, new missions opportunities, building projects, or some other special ministries to give to. Watching our money make a difference is a reward in itself. As we give, we always remember that we are "sowing seed" into people and ministries that will reap a harvest. Part of this harvest, Paul said in Philippians 4:17 is "credited to our account" in heaven, too!

Remember your motives. The materialistic urges of modern society continually wear at the foundations of a God-given desire to make giving a top priority. That's why you must keep two reasons to give in the forefront of your consciousness.

First, remember tithes and offerings are a doorway to God's blessing. His desire is to pour out blessings from heaven (Malachi 3:10), to give back to you a "good measure, pressed down, shaken together and running over"

(Luke 6:38), and to meet all of your needs (Philippians 4:19). God warned his people, "You will sow much seed in the field but you will harvest little, because locusts will devour it" (Deuteronomy 28:38). Refuse to let Satan steal your joy or your blessing. Keep the channel of God's blessing open.

Second, remember tithes and offerings are a tremendous checkpoint to monitor the level of your obedience. Tithing is not the end of our commitment to God in our giving. Personal ministry is God's plan. Paul reminds Timothy,

> Command those who are rich in this present world not to be arrogant nor to put their hope in wealth, which is so uncertain, but to put their hope in God, who richly provides us with everything for our enjoyment. Command them to do good, to be rich in good deeds, and to be generous and willing to share (1 Timothy 6:17, 18).

As you determine that you want to "give to get to give again" God will bring more and more people and needs into your life for you to touch financially. Resist the temptation to write these requests off as "black holes," always seeking more. Instead, pray over each opportunity and ask yourself the question, Is God bringing this need into my life to help me grow in faith and service? If he is, you will already have the habit built into your spending patterns which allows you to obey out of generosity and love.

In 1995 members of a church in Boulder, Colorado, surprised their community and made national headlines. One afternoon they went to a trailer park in a poverty-stricken part of town to hand out free hot dogs. Along with the food was the biggest surprise—they brought their Sunday morning offering of $80,000 to give away! Congregational leaders visited every family in the park to assess their needs, then they shared the money through vouchers or checks for specific needs. The preacher, James Ryle, described the church's gift to the residents of the trailer park as a "hand up" rather than a handout.

Giving like this is bound to please God's heart. We can cultivate this kind of giving in our own congregations when we personally decide to accept the privilege and responsibility for managing our own share of God's resources. Experience the excitement of taking God at his word!

Notes:

[1]Del Rogers, *Stewardship Enrichment*. (Dallas: The Rogers Company). Used by permission.

Think It Through
Word Three: I Trust You to Manage Material Resources

1. How often does your current approach to giving match the decisions suggested in this chapter?

2. As you read these three passages, focus on the attitudes you think God wants his children to develop. List as many as you can.

    Malachi 3:10

Luke 6:38

2 Corinthians 9:6-12

3. Word Three encourages you to make three decisions. Read each decision and circle the number, from 1 (never) to 10 (always), that best describes your current giving practices.

   Decision 1—Give to the Lord this Sunday.

   1   2   3   4   5   6   7   8   9   10

   Decision 2—Give to the Lord every Sunday.

   1   2   3   4   5   6   7   8   9   10

   Decision 3—Plan to give "tithes and offerings."

   1   2   3   4   5   6   7   8   9   10

4. James 1:5 tells us that if we ask God for wisdom he will give it generously. Take time now to ask God to grant you wisdom in your giving decisions. Listen for the new wisdom that God will provide.

Meditate on God's Word

Luke 16:10, 11

Whoever can be trusted with very little can also be trusted with much, and whoever is dishonest with very little will also be dishonest with much. So if you have not been trustworthy in handling worldly wealth, who will trust you with true riches?

1 Corinthians 16:1, 2

Now about the collection for God's people: Do what I told the Galatian churches to do. On the first day of every week, each one of you should set aside a sum of money in keeping with his income, saving it up, so that when I come no collections will have to be made.

2 Corinthians 8:1-9

And now, brothers, we want you to know about the grace that God has given the Macedonian churches. Out of the most severe trial, their overflowing joy and their extreme poverty welled up in rich generosity. For I testify that they gave as much as they were able, and even beyond their ability. Entirely on their own, they urgently pleaded with us for the privilege of sharing in this service to the saints. And they did not do as we expected, but they gave themselves first to the Lord and then to us in keeping with God's will. So we urged Titus, since he had earlier made a beginning, to bring also to completion this act of grace on your part. But just as you excel in everything—in faith, in speech, in knowledge, in complete earnestness and in your love for us—see that you also excel in this grace of giving.

I am not commanding you, but I want to test the sincerity of your love by comparing it with the earnestness of others. For you know the grace of our Lord Jesus Christ, that though he was rich, yet for your sakes he became poor, so that you through his poverty might become rich.

Titus 3:14

Our people must learn to devote themselves to doing what is good, in order that they may provide for daily necessities and not live unproductive lives.

Isn't it a privilege to be a trusted manager for Almighty God? That's what you are! And God wants to empower you to become even more trustworthy. Step out in faith. God will meet you!

Let's Pray ...

Dear God, when it comes to my giving, I don't want to be like flint or a sponge. Lord help me become a honeycomb! Teach me to give without fear that I'll run out of your supply. Build my character so that giving the firstfruits of all my income will become as natural to me as breathing. Your kingdom and your glory are what I want to live for! In view of a returning Savior, I pray in Jesus' name. Amen.

2 Corinthians 8:7

But just as you excel in everything—in faith, in speech, in knowledge, in complete earnestness and in your love for us—see that you also excel in this grace of giving.

In the next few pages you'll discover:

❖   It's vital to keep growing in your giving.

❖   God is at work today in the lives of those who take him at his word.

❖   God works through you—especially when you give in faith.

WORD FOUR:

I Will Help You Give More Than You Can Imagine

Several years ago, I sat in the car talking with one of my older Christian friends after a lunch meeting. As the conversation moved toward giving, this wise, godly brother made a surprising comment. He told me, "When my wife and I got married, I decided we should grow in our giving until we could give over 50 percent to the Lord." I'll admit I thought that was impossible, if not down right crazy! Then my friend said, "It took us a few years, but you know what? We made it!" This man wasn't wealthy when he decided to put God first in his giving, either. As time went by, though, he received numerous promotions, which resulted in a prominent position with a major retailing firm.

First, the Lord gave him the desire to be generous, then he gave him blessings to match.

We need to hear more stories of faithful devotion to God which will encourage us to stretch higher in our giving and to trust him to provide the harvest.

Setting a Faith Budget

Well-known author Henry Blackaby has greatly impacted my thinking and teaching on giving. The following story illustrates his insight:

> One year the people on our finance committee said, "You have taught us to walk by faith in every area of the life of our church except in the budget." I asked them to explain. They said, "Well, when we set the budget, we set the budget on the basis of what we believe we can do. It does not reflect that we expect God to do anything."
>
> "Hummm," I said. "Then how do you feel we ought to set the budget?"
>
> They said, "First, we ought to determine all that God wants to do through us. Second, we need to put down what that will cost. Then we need to divide the budget goal into three categories: (1) what we plan to do through our tithes; (2) what others have promised to do; and (3) what we must depend on God to do."
>
> As a church we prayed and decided God wanted us to use this approach to budgeting. We did not try to dream our own dreams for God. We had to be absolutely sure God was leading us to do the things we put in the budget. Then we listed what that would cost. We listed what we thought our people would give and what others had said they would give. The difference between

what we could reasonably expect to receive and the total was what we would ask God to provide.

The big question was: What is our operating budget? Well, by faith we adopted the grand total as our operating budget. At this point we reached a crisis of belief. Did we really believe that the God who led us to do these things also would provide the resources to bring them to pass? Anytime God leads you to do something that has God-sized dimensions, you will face a crisis of belief. When you face a crisis of belief, what you do next reveals what you really believe about God.

The budget of our church normally would have been $74,000. The budget we set was $164,000. We pledged to pray daily that God would meet our needs. Any money that came in that we did not anticipate we credited to God. At the end of the year we had received $172,000. God taught our church a lesson in faith that radically changed us all.[1]

That story didn't just change the members of that church, it changed me, too! These people gave more than they imagined they could. They honestly, prayerfully, and sincerely sought the Lord's will, even though their decisions caused a "crisis of belief." They learned that they would have to trust God to provide an amount far beyond what their experiences told them was possible. Then they decided to trust God, and God didn't let them down.

Are you going through a personal crisis of belief with your finances? If so, this discomfort may be God's way of getting your attention. As you prepare to receive the harvest God has promised you, you'll have to come face to face with the obstacles blocking your faith. Just like the people in Blackaby's story, you can lean on God in prayer and follow through as he leads you.

The teaching and encouragement in this book is aimed at one central truth: You can trust God's word. When the Lord of the universe promises us anything, have no fear or doubt; his word will come to pass.

It is crucial for us to get the truths of God's great promises of provision implanted firmly into our minds and hearts. When they are, Satan will be disarmed. Both disobedience and fear, two of his most frequently used weapons, will lose their impact, and the work of expanding the Kingdom of Jesus will surge forward.

We must act in faith first and then expect God to honor his word. It is similar to the example recorded in 2 Kings 3:9-20. The armies of Israel, Judah, and Edom were allied together in battle with the nation of Moab. During the course of one of their marches to engage the Moabites, the armies ran out of water for the men and their pack animals. The three kings met together to consider their options. King Jehoshaphat led the other two kings to visit the prophet Elisha and ask him for counsel from the Lord. Elisha responded, "This is what the LORD says: You will see neither wind nor rain, yet this valley will be filled with water, and you, your cattle and your other animals will drink. This is an easy thing in the eyes of the LORD; he will also hand Moab over to you."

The armies followed Elisha's unusual instructions from God. They dug dry ditches and waited for God to fill them miraculously with water. The story continues, "The next morning, about the time for offering the sacrifice, there it was—water flowing from the direction of Edom! And the land was filled with water" (v. 20). Notice their faith in God to do something beyond their normal experience. Notice also the importance of the number of ditches they dug.

Evidently, they dug lots of ditches because the land was "filled with water." The Lord had promised to fill every ditch they chose to dig, and he kept his promise.

What do you think would have happened if they had dug only a few ditches? Clearly, the Lord would have filled them, but the people would have missed the full blessing God intended. Do you see the point? When God tells us to be generous (1 Timothy 6:18) or to excel in the grace of giving (2 Corinthians 8:7), he is actually giving us an opportunity to "dig ditches" for him to fill today. How many ditches are you digging? Your answer is evidence of how much belief you have in him to fulfill all his promises, whether spiritual, physical, or emotional.

Our role is to follow Jesus, just like Peter did in Luke 5. Peter and his fishing partners had fished all night and failed to catch anything. After Jesus finished a morning of teaching, he told them to head back out into the deep water and drop their nets again and expect a catch. Peter's conventional wisdom told him that going out again would be a waste of time. After all, they were experienced fishermen who had worked hard all night and failed to catch even a single fish! But his respect for Jesus caused him to consent. He told the Lord, "Because you say so, I will let down the nets" (Luke 5:5). The men pulled in a haul of fish so large their nets began to break! All this occurred because Peter took the Lord at his word. When God makes a promise he always comes through, often in remarkable ways.

Here's the bottom line: God is in the people business! More than anything he wants us to become like his Son, Jesus. To do this he will love us, bless us, discipline us, and develop us, by the power of his Holy Spirit, so that we become all he wants us to be. After all, this is entirely for our own good. So experience the joy of generosity. Practice growing in the power of giving. Take God at his word. You *will* experience the power of giving.

Notes:

[1]Henry Blackaby and Claude King, *Experiencing God: Knowing and Doing the Will of God* (Nashville: LifeWay Press, 1990), p. 108. All rights reserved. Used by permission.

Think It Through
Word Four: I Will Help You Give More Than You Can Imagine

1. Imagine yourself as a member of the congregation in Henry Blackaby's story. Would your response to the committee's decision create a "crisis of belief" for you? Why?

2. What personal crisis of belief are you experiencing today? Pray for God's guidance to handle them.

3. Identify at least four attitudes about giving that God wants you to change. Pray about any barriers preventing your changes.

Meditate on God's Word

2 Corinthians 8:9-11

For you know the grace of our Lord Jesus Christ, that though he was rich, yet for your sakes he became poor, so that you through his poverty might become rich.

And here is my advice about what is best for you in this matter: Last year you were the first not only to give but also to have the desire to do so. Now finish the work, so that your eager willingness to do it may be matched by your completion of it, according to your means.

2 Corinthians 9:6, 7

Remember this: Whoever sows sparingly will also reap sparingly, and whoever sows generously will also reap generously. Each man should give what he has decided in his heart to give, not reluctantly or under compulsion, for God loves a cheerful giver.

Galatians 6:9, 10

Let us not become weary in doing good, for at the proper time we will reap a harvest if we do not give up. Therefore, as we have opportunity, let us do good to all people, especially to those who belong to the family of believers.

Ephesians 3:20, 21

Now to him who is able to do immeasurably more

than all we ask or imagine, according to his power that is at work within us, to him be glory in the church and in Christ Jesus throughout all generations, for ever and ever! Amen.

How deeply do you desire the rewards God gives to his faithful, generous followers? Will you accept the challenge the Lord has laid on your heart?

Let's Pray ...

Heavenly Father, I sense these lessons have provided me with a fresh awareness of blessings from your hand. Now it's time for me to take a step up in my willingness to take you at your word. Please grant me the grace to stand in the riches of your provision and stretch to become like your Son. I realize he became poor for my sake, and I have access to all your riches. What a precious reality! I will praise you and thank you forever! By Jesus' power and love, I pray. Amen.

About the Author

Dr. Kregg Hood, author, speaker, and educator, is executive vice president for Sweet Publishing. Dr. Hood has also served as a minister, a missionary, and a college instructor.

Hood earned his doctorate from Texas Tech University in instructional communication in 1987. He also holds master's degrees in missions and in religious communication and a bachelor of arts degree with undergraduate majors in Bible, biblical languages, and mathematics.

He and his wife, Karen, are parents of a daughter, Kalah, and a son, Kyle.

Dr. Hood is available to teach or speak for special events and may be contacted by phone, 1-800-531-5220, or by fax, 1-817-232-2030.

Thank You for Reading *Take God at His Word*

This book is part of a comprehensive teaching plan which helps church leaders teach their congregations to trust God with their finances.

The *Take God at His Word* study program takes a significantly different approach from most stewardship series:

1. It is distinctly positive. Learning to give to God is an exciting adventure, filled with blessings.

2. It focuses directly on building genuine trust in God. This study is more about faith than about finances.

3. The strong, practical preaching and daily, personal, in-depth study work together to cultivate an environment of faith and motivation which leads to action.

To find out about the complete *Take God at His Word* teaching plan, call toll-free 877-TAKE-GOD or click on www.TakeGod.com.